T0149509

He's Not Like Us.
His Kick Was Special.

ROY BAXTER. III

WESTBOW
PRESS®
A DIVISION OF THOMAS NELSON
& ZONDERVAN

WestBow Press books may be ordered through booksellers or by contacting:

WestBow Press
A Division of Thomas Nelson & Zondervan
1663 Liberty Drive
Bloomington, IN 47403
www.westbowpress.com
1 (866) 928-1240

Because of the dynamic nature of the Internet, any web addresses or
links contained in this book may have changed since publication and
may no longer be valid. The views expressed in this work are solely those
of the author and do not necessarily reflect the views of the publisher,
and the publisher hereby disclaims any responsibility for them.

Any people depicted in stock imagery provided by Thinkstock are models,
and such images are being used for illustrative purposes only.
Certain stock imagery © Thinkstock.

ISBN: 978-1-5127-7703-1 (sc)
ISBN: 978-1-5127-7702-4 (e)

Library of Congress Control Number: 2017902974

Print information available on the last page.

WestBow Press rev. date: 03/29/2017

Credits:

Book Cover Graphic Artist
Mr. Matthew Drummond

Technical Advisor
Mr. Lester Jordan

Typist/Consultant/Editor
Mrs. Vickie M. Culver

Back Cover Photo
Ms. Ashlee M. Culver

In Loving Memory of

Mother Gardner

and

Victoria L. Herbert-Moore

PROLOGUE

Can anything good come from that terrible city called Newark, New Jersey, where a large number of African Americans reside?

Yes, without a doubt. What the Creator has in store for us is truly remarkable. No opposition on earth can stand in the way if he has something special for you to accomplish. Lack of wealth is really not that big a deal.

A sizable number of people live in the northeast quadrant of these United States. To stand out or be recognized in a particular area of expertise is a daunting task. Who has the critical eye, and why can't they see? Another one has shot up into the atmosphere.

In earlier decades, African Americans migrated to the northern cities to find employment. People of color had a realistic understanding that if they worked hard, they could at the very least make a living. Generally, people worked very hard during the day. Once that powerful sun set, it was a whole other ball game.

New York City's biggest and brightest stars showcased their talents across the waters. New Jersey's most-populated city was the serious after-party place to be. Other cities or towns could show you a good time, but Newark was the party town. The jazz clubs and night life were second to none.

People kept coming to Newark, and the city kept growing. The Irish resided in the Vailsburg section; West Ward housed the Irish and the Italians. East Ward housed the Portuguese; South Ward housed the Jewish and African Americans. North Ward housed Italians, African Americans, and Spanish people. Central Ward also housed the Jewish and African Americans. Generally, people felt comfortable in their established communities. If you were found to be in the wrong part of town, that might be somewhat of a problem.

Newark was a boxing town, and it inspired many great boxing legends. Many young men wanted to acquire that sweet science and skill. Throughout the city were a good number of boxing gyms to visit. High school athletes were pretty diversified within a wide range of sports. Some of the high schools had pretty good wrestling programs. That being said, there could be no mistake—boxing had center stage.

How you carried yourself was always important. Even on a good day sometimes you just could not avoid a fight. A group of young people might be messing around and having fun; somewhere in the crowd curiosity about who could whip who would circulate. People in the crowd might start to think too hard about the outcome of a particular match up, yet they were too afraid to fight themselves. The instigator would place an object on someone's shoulder and say, "If John knocks that top off your shoulder, that would be your mother." John would push the top off, and then it was usually on. The crowd would make plenty of space so they wouldn't miss the action.

A young man with pretty good skills didn't have to fight all the time. Sometimes his hands could make the argument that he wasn't one you wanted to mess with.

Who could see what was about to happen? A foreign invasion was about to hit the community. William A. Wilson, James Cheetim,

Allan Lee, Shaffer, Angelines, and Maggie were some of the early pioneers. Decades later, these gentlemen would be recognized as the patriarchs of martial arts in the greater Newark area. They served as the foundational pillars and unveiled a sensational and complete fighting machine—right smack in the middle of the 1950s. During that time, an exciting idea came to fruition. The first African American karate dojo opened its doors. Back in the States after his military training in Osaka, Japan, Grand Master Wilson opened a school of martial arts in the year of 1956.

A small number of men had acquired martial arts training while serving in the US military. Grand Master Wilson turned his vision into a reality and established the first American dojo in the city of Newark. After a few years, he had four schools operating out of the five wards in Newark. Master Cheetim and Master Allan Lee would share a space together on Broad Street downtown. People were exhilarated and gung ho to see more of this great art form. This phenomenon was taking firm root within the community. They would teach their students to uphold high standards of excellence and maintain good moral character.

Kung fu master Allan Lee broke tradition with his Asian colleagues. The Chinese art was not taught to ethnic groups outside of their own. This was truly unusual.

A year or so went by. Then Ronnie Gardner was born on June 30, 1957. His father was of Cuban decent. His mother was young and hardworking, and she dedicated her life to providing for and raising her family. In a couple of years, Ronnie would be joined by two little sisters. In the mid-1960s, Ronnie and his family moved to Schuyler Avenue in the Weequahic section of the South Ward in Newark. His education began at Hawthorne Avenue Elementary School.

Hoping that life would improve for the next generation, Ronnie's parents shielded the children from the harsh realities of that era. The NAACP, along with other civil rights organizations, fought a great many battles on our behalf. Back in the day we were referred to as colored people or Negroes, and utterances like that would cut right to the bone marrow. Years later we would embrace the term African Americans.

Hawthorne Avenue Elementary School

A charismatic, young, exciting fighter came along. He gripped the nation by its throat and said it was a new day. Things would be changing. His name was Cassius Clay, a youthful, flashy fighter who burst onto the scene in the early 1960s. He became a favorite in every city throughout the United States. He spoke rather boastfully and had crazy skills that were unequaled. Boxing had someone for many to love—and he was also someone for others to hate. Ronnie would get to see a young African American man who displayed a good deal of backbone. His love and level of commitment to his people were refreshing and influential. Cassius Clay changed his name to Muhammad Ali. He also had a desire to change his religion. He would become an African American Muslim, a new member of the Nation of Islam. In the midst of the civil rights struggles, the Nation of Islam set out on a different road.

Dr. Martin Luther King Jr. was another strong voice on the scene during the turbulent times. A young Baptist minister thrust into a leadership role, he had a broad set of shoulders. His foes were evil-spirited men who wore white hoods, as well as countless other members of racist institutions. In the 1960s, many brutal acts of hatred were carried out against people of color. At a church in Birmingham, Alabama, four little girls were killed by a bomb.

A powerful leader who would command worldwide attention was Malcolm X. He let it be known that we were a peaceful people, but the constant turning of the other cheek wasn't working for us **"By any means necessary."** Many years later, people all around the world would come to embrace that sentiment. In 1965 he was slain. One and one weren't adding up to two. Our government leaders spoke about the fifty states being unified. Nothing could be further from the truth. Civil rights champions were being killed one after another. Police brutality was a huge deal on the minds of many living in the inner cities. A few months earlier in Watts, California, there had been a riot. Tension was at an all-time high. Almost any little thing could become a trigger point and set things off.

A rumor about a cab driver who was savagely beaten by the police ran through the city of Newark at breakneck speed. No one gave us a heads-up about what was about to happen. Folks started losing their minds. In the Central Ward, stores were looted, buildings were set ablaze, and then the unthinkable—a small number of white people were said to have been attacked. As the media began to broadcast some of these images, the lightning rod was the physical attacks against the Caucasians. A lot of negative things could happen to Negroes or colored men anywhere in America. On the black-and-white televisions across the nation, the accounts of whites being battered were all that really mattered. Seeing people carrying sofa beds and washing machines on their backs was insignificant. Early on, the Newark Police Department realized that they were not in control of the situation. We were in a state of emergency, and the New Jersey National Guard was called upon. The invention of the cell phone would not happen for decades; however, you could almost believe that folks had some kind of futuristic device to get the word out.

More than one hundred cities across our great land were in a state of crisis. A curfew was put into place, and everyone had to remain indoors. Everything came to a halt. The situation was extremely dangerous. The biggest burden landed on the shoulders of parents. They had to forcefully keep their children from looking out of the windows, to save them from being shot. Some men, women, and children were shot and killed. From a little kid's perspective, living through this experience became something you would never forget!

CHAPTER 1

A young family man lived on Hillside Avenue in the South Ward. His mother lived approximately ten minutes away by car in the Central Ward. Word reached him that his brother had been arrested in the mayhem. He was deeply concerned about his mom's health and the stresses she might be weathering. Before he could get off Hillside Ave, his car was stopped by a New Jersey National Guardsman. The Guardsman was heated, and he shouted furiously at the young man. In an intense state of rage he yelled, "Get out of that car! We are under orders to shoot and kill anyone we deem to be a threat. That means men, women, or children! I don't care anything about you trying to reach your mother! You will have to continue to your trip on foot. Young man, understand this; this car is staying put! Before you make it to where you're heading, you'll probably be shot to death. Get on your way, and may your God be with you." The grace of God was with him, and he reached his destination safely. Generally when big events come around, you feel like there ought to be someone on standby to sound an alarm.

Especially in the Central Ward, Newark looked like a war-torn city. The devastation was like nothing you could really imagine. Within day's right after the riots, the Caucasian people began abruptly migrating out of Newark.

People were scared to death; the curfew was still in place. Miss Gardner, along with the many thousands of other parents, was very

1

effective in carrying the reality of the life-threatening situation at hand. The gritty, harsh streets of Newark had nothing on this sudden flash riot. Who could really be prepared for something explosive like this to happen? The city of nearly four hundred thousand people was on a crazy lockdown. The riot that had sparked in Newark set off an inconceivable chain of events. More than one hundred urban cities throughout our nation collectively spoke with one voice. African Americans were conscious of our harsh existence and the many acts of brutality committed against us. Young people did not want to hear what their parents had heard: "Just be a little patient."

After the riots, when opportunity allowed you could see the devastation. Businesses closed down or burned down, trash filled the streets, and many eyes held a look of total disbelief. The Newark public schools faced a tall order: to bring back some sense of normalcy so the thousands of students could finish out the rest of the school year.

Some young men wanted fresh new names to mark a new beginning for themselves. Islam was the path they would begin to travel. Ronnie exercised his right to travel that different road. Muslims wanted to shed the slave names given to them by their slave masters. The sexual exploits of European males against women of African American decent were too much. Ronnie became Raheem Ali Gardner.

From the late 1960s to mid-1970s there was an explosion in Islamic representation. It seemed as if everyone wanted to be a Muslim. People adopted names left and right: Shabazz, Muhammad, anything but keeping the slave names given to them at birth. A lot of ex-cons fresh out of prison were on the streets teaching Islam. The greater Tri-State Islamic community was pushing the ideas of black-owned businesses, which was not a new concept but now an idea that people were ready to employ. Muhammad speaks. Newspapers were sold, bean pies were sold, and people were excited by the talk of unity. Muslim men called the black-woman their "queens." A lot of the right things were being said; young people had an alternative outside Christianity.

Raheem would sometimes attend the mosque in New York City. In Newark, it was either Temple 25A on South Orange Avenue or Temple B on Bergen Street and Lehigh Avenue Islam was providing him with supportive messages and a good deal of self-pride.

Newark was an unbelievably territorial, divided city. A silent message permeated the entire city. If someone looked, acted, or smelled like a Muslim, they were not to come under any kind of attack. The fear of free movement was something that no one could truly deny. The entire Muslim community in the greater Newark area benefited immensely from the social decree that was put into effect.

Regardless of the great numbers of people going through changes, there was indeed structure in the household. Bedtime was roughly round about nine at night. Television executives competed fiercely for people to be parked and watching their TV show. Youngsters were targeted between the hours of four in the afternoon and nine and enjoyed watching *Batman*. One show in particular became an amazing success.

The new TV show was called the *Green Hornet*, featuring crime fighters and a young Asian guy who could lay someone out in an amazing heart beat. The masked character named Kato was the Green Hornet's sidekick. He wore a mask and became much bigger than the star of the show. When he was engaged in a fight scene, no one thought about turning the dial. The actor's name was Bruce Lee. The fight scenes were short and riveting, sure to keep you glued to that seat. Bruce Lee would become responsible for boosting the interest in martial arts. He set the stage for much bigger things that would soon follow.

After the show, young people talked about this mysterious "karate thing," so to speak. Not only was it a hit in America but also in Hong Kong and the entire Asian world. In the Tri-State area, advertisers even promoted a Green Hornet shoe. Some teenagers did pay the quarter for bus fare to travel to downtown Newark and purchase the Green Hornet shoe.

Bruce Lee was red hot. And then, all of a sudden, he vanished into thin air.

Utopia was in the air for thousands of young sisters, not only African American girls but girls of all races. A Caucasian gentleman named Ed Sullivan had a popular variety show. He would showcase up and coming new talent. Five young men appeared on the black-and-white TV, calling themselves the Jackson Five. Wearing big afros and bell-bottom pants, they could sing and dance. It didn't hurt that they were good-looking young men. They were an overnight sensation. The television ratings went through the roof. Many young men were envious of Michael Jackson, but they would never admit to it. The girls loved those young men, especially Michael. Boys from all over the fifty states felt the same thing: "Hey, Michael, leave some girls for us. It's not right. You have all the girls."

On the other end of the spectrum was Brother Marvin Gaye singing "What's Going On." His song helped raise the consciousness of our nation.

While attending Hawthorne Avenue School, Raheem understood that his grammar school education lacked the quality and properties he would later need. In his heart he knew that he was just getting by. There were a lot of choices confronting him and decisions to be made. He decided to keep on the martial arts path and see where it might take him. He loved the martial arts, primarily for self-defense. After two years of training under Sensei Bozc, Raheem would routinely hear people say things like, "Hey, man, you're pretty good at this karate thing."

In sparring competitions Raheem won his bouts but without any real sense of confidence. He competed at the Newark Boys Club on Hawthorne Avenue, not far from where he lived. He and the other up-and-coming local martial artists appeared at Newark's Symphony Hall, Boys Club locations, and at many types of recreational venues.

Sensei Bozc was accessible to the point of pure absurdity. The dojo was open six out of seven days a week until nine at night during the school week and all day Saturday until late. During the summer months, it was almost always open, except on Sundays. Raheem routinely said that they spent so much time at the dojo that they had no choice but to be good. He said if you weren't improving as a martial artist, then maybe you should consider doing something else.

Mr. Bozc occasionally told Raheem that karate was much more than kicks, punches, or blocks. With dedication, hard training, and focus, karate was a special vehicle that could take him places. He heard the words without thinking too deeply about what was being said.

Master Bozc was a good mentor for those without a role model around on a regular basis, a very positive influence on the students who showed interest in learning. His approach was very professional, with a strong sense of business. Not many people could say they ever saw him without his black briefcase. No one knew what was in that portable case, but it was always with him. As in other urban cities, the Newark experience was capable of steering a youth in a wide range of directions. Much to Master Bozc's credit, his students appreciated the many hours of martial arts training they received. Martial arts became their choice, and it was more than enough to keep them out of many kinds of trouble. Trouble and ill-fated consequences weren't always the jewelry one had to wear.

Roy Baxter. III

Around 1968 and 1969 the social fabric of the inner city became an eye opener. The young people who were drafted to fight a war started returning home. Well-to-do and rich people had managed to keep their children out of the Vietnamese war. Some came home with missing limbs. A good portion of them had psychological difficulties. Alcohol and drug dependency became the norm. These chemical means were used to combat the complexities and cruelty of the Vietnam War. A universal understanding was accepted in the minds of many young people, the simple fact that older people liked to drink and get drunk.

All of sudden, little ones began to witness people in their early twenties ingesting a variety of chemicals to become high. It was a confusing and puzzling time in our nation's history. Adding to the craziness of the situation, youngsters saw kids and teenagers out and about selling drugs. The trend seemed to come from out of nowhere. The next phase was hearing about the drug overdoses taking place. All of this was a bit much to absorb. One day Raheem was a little kid trying to navigate his way through life, and now he had some serious choices to make. *Do I stay away from drugs or do I seek that feeling that others often talk about?*

At the age of thirteen, Raheem experienced getting high from smoking marijuana. Like many good parents, Ms. Gardner had no knowledge of her son's experimentation. One particular evening she was walking home from her job at Beth Israel Hospital, which was down the street and around the corner from where they lived. When she walked up to the car Raheem was sitting in, she could barely see who was sitting there. Earlier he and an older gentleman had smoked plenty of marijuana and then simply fell asleep. She knocked on the car window; he woke up and opened the car door. When the door opened, the odor was strong, and smoke escaped into the atmosphere. She was very angry and let them have a piece of her mind. Whether or not it was comfortable for parents to believe, the truth was that a majority of youngsters were curious about drugs.

Attending Hawthorne Avenue School was a crazy proposition in itself. In the simple act of just coming home from school, he was subject to being jumped. He lived on Schuyler Avenue, and conflict would often arise between his street and Hawthorne Avenue. The street he had to cross to reach school and return home was a reoccurring problem. Usually after school, someone would yell down the block, "Hawthorne Avenue is here, and we are ready to fight"!

Mom would say, "Raheem, I need you to go the store and get me a Pepsi and a pack of Newport cigarettes." His thinking cap had to go on. Simple travel required a strategy. The streets he traveled weren't far, but the route had to be correct.

As crazy as Newark could seem at times, it was also a pretty amazing town to grow up in. During the hot summer, he could walk over to the John F. Kennedy swimming pool in the heart of the Central Ward. The newly constructed pool was spacious and beautiful. From various communities from around the city, on very hot days the kids would come and find relief.

Raheem felt very fortunate about the days he went to the JFK swimming pool. A good many youths could not say the same thing. When leaving the swimming facility, some had to part with their money, or perhaps an article of clothing. The thugs who preyed on others would normally start with what was on your feet. The must-have sneakers of the day were Chuck Taylor's Converse. The sneakers were so popular that many prayers were sent up by children, hoping that a pair might fit in their family's budget. The sneakers cost $10.00. In the late 1960s that was a lot of money. Ten dollars during that era is equivalent to $110.00 today.

After swimming you might follow up with a group of guys to play basketball at Chancellor Avenue School or maybe a football game at Weequahic High School's Uttermans Field. In the evening you could catch a cool breeze; someone would bring out a record player in a small box. You could place a nickel or quarter on an arm to keep it steady on a 45-rpm record. Every week you could expect that some singing artist would release a possible hit record. A number of record labels were putting out some unbelievable muscle, but Motown was the legendary hit maker. Great music could be heard on the radio on WNJR, 1430 on the AM dial, and WBLS, 107.5 on the FM dial.

Raheem had the distinction of living from the eighth grade to grade twelve in one of the most prolific party epicenters one could imagine. In the Weequahic section in the South Ward, from March to until November you could go to multiple house parties, from one to four every weekend. If you wanted to have a good time, you got the address, dressed to impress, and made your way there. In the Central Ward toward downtown, there was a teenage club on Clinton Avenue called the Ebony Manor. DJ Slim, a member of Mark 4 Disco, provided the cutting-edge music and equipment that would launch us out of orbit of soul music.

On another scorching day, some kids took the caps of the fire hydrants and added a strainer so it would spray wildly. It was a lot of fun and laughs. Seeing the girls' underwear beneath their wet clothing was an added bonus for the boys.

Clean, pressed clothing was very important back in the day. Parents wanted their kids to look good and have a life greater than they'd experienced. You could ride a bus to downtown Newark for twenty-five cents. On Market Street you could go into the Universal Men and Boys shop. Twenty dollars got you a nice pair of pants and a pretty decent dress shirt.

For young men, every two weeks or so a haircut was in order. The neighborhood barber was fairly close to where he lived. There was always a bunch of people there for the same routine. Everyone felt they had the best barber. You sat down and waited your turn to have your hair cut. Everyone kept a mental count of who was next. As a maturing young man, Raheem appreciated the importance of grooming. A young lady might not have the greatest instincts of what to look for in a man, but nevertheless she wanted him to look good! At the barbershop the conversation could become very hot and stimulating. The older gentlemen would educate the younger and dissect the social landscape, both local and national. Walking down the street afterward, he looked good and was a little more informed about his world.

On Saturday mornings, the long day could not start before Raheem, Sheila, and Stacey completed their house chores. After the house was cleaned he took his little sisters for bike rides or developed his martial art. For a period of time a nagging thought lingered in the mind of young Gardner. *How in the world am I going to protect me and my two little sisters? I'm short, slender build and these streets in Newark are unforgiving.*

Mom was about tough love. She gave whatever she had. If she didn't have it, she would let you know it. She did not promise something she wasn't able to make good on. "Raheem, I don't have it. I'm doing the best I can. If that isn't good enough for you, then I don't know what to tell you. You gonna have to do what you have to do." She said that pretty often: "Raheem, do what you have to do." He'd get pretty angry and ask, "Ma, what you mean by that?" He wasn't quite sure about the precise message that was intended. "I don't have the money for the sneakers, so you gonna have to what you gotta do." His feelings would be a little hurt. "Ma, what are you saying? Where are you coming from?"

CHAPTER 2

Irvington Technical High School was a high school that let you know there were other options for you. Not everyone was going to go off to college. For half of the school day it offered the regular academic courses that most high schools taught. The second portion of the day students focused on the trade they'd selected to learn. At Irvington Tech School a typical morning included math, science, health. There were upper-classmen around, but the new boys were concerned with their status. After so many years in elementary school they had a few statements to make. "We are here, and we are different from other freshman classes."

There was indeed something special about this class of students, who came into the school with a chip on their collective shoulders. You would be hard pressed to know that they were freshmen. The upper-classmen knew who we were. We walked and strutted like sophomores or juniors.

In the time between classes, a trend started to emerge. A few boxers put in some work between classes. The feel was almost like that of a boxing club. Between classes they could forget they were at school. In comparison to other high schools the tech school was quite small, with a population of about four hundred students. The freshman totaled about 120 or so. Throughout the day, the five percent who just loved the sweet art of boxing went at it.

Two days a week there was gym. After exercising and warming up, there was plenty of basketball. Irvington Tech was no joke when it came to the basketball program. Lunch was right after gym. Some students ate out, and others ate in the cafeteria. Friday was the day when most students ate in school. The cafeteria offered macaroni and cheese, along with fish. The other days you could take or leave the food there. The last four hours of the day were devoted to learning a trade. The school day seemed like any other at first. In the sheet metal shop, there was a door at the back of the room that led to a fairly large drafting room. At the back end of this room was a cage where tools would be stored, shaped very much like an octagon. It was an ideal space to polish boxing skills. For whatever reason, the air in the room was a little different. Inside the cage were about twelve people, with six people boxing. Soon the martial artists in the cage sort of exploded, as if they were saying, "Fellas, we got this." It was so different than anything that had been happening. Electricity was definitely in the atmosphere. A brother nicknamed "Ears" wore his kung fu uniform and demonstrated a Chinese form. Most of the guys who participated in this exhibition had decent levels of skill and execution.

At that precise moment my right eye caught a quick frame. In a fraction of a second I saw a dynamic kick shoot up, twelve o'clock high. That brother was not like us—that kick was special! It spoke to expertise and separation in comparison to our kicks. It happened in a microsecond, but my brain processed the information thoroughly. Young Raheem Gardner was the truth. This gift-wrapped Asian treasure lured us in. He dared to go in much deeper than what we saw on the surface. All in, holding nothing back, he tapped into his soul.

Everyone took to Raheem's warm and quiet spirit.

His main inner circle included Dexter, Willie, Tony, and Jimmy. Easygoing and somewhat quiet, he could coexist with any and all types of personalities. Although freshmen problems would arise, no one seemed to bother him. Tool and die was the trade that he'd entered the school to learn. Later he transferred to the machine shop. His teacher was Mr. Drew. Every now and then, not often, Raheem would come off as if he were a bad boy. Mr. Drew saw right through that and paid him no mind. Mr. Drew looked him square in the face on a few occasions and said, "You gonna be somebody one day."

One of those days came along that you just couldn't foresee. Raheem and his buddies were looking out the shop window and saw a young man walking down the street alongside his girlfriend. Without the teacher's knowledge, they were smoking marijuana in the shop.

"Raheem, this dude is with your girl. He must be snatching her up." Raheem got angry, worked up over what was being said. Raheem and the fellows snuck out of class to confront the young man. Raheem was in hot pursuit. He was high and very agitated. Running frantically, Johnny's footing was unstable. On the edge of a curb he began to fall. At about the same time Raheem leaped up and executed a double front kick. Loud voices cried, "Leave him alone, Raheem!" The kick made contact. As Johnny flew forward in the middle of the cul-de-sac, his face hit a willow tree. The force and trauma knocked him out cold, splitting his forehead, breaking his nose, pushing his teeth backward into his mouth, busting both lower and upper lips. It was a terrible scene. Raheem and his friends were nervous, and they ran back to Irvington Tech as if nothing had even happened.

Sixth period rolled around, and an announcement came over the school's loudspeaker.

"Will Ronnie Gardner, Willie, Tony, and Jimmy all report to the guidance counselors' office." Irvington police and detectives were downstairs in the office. The boys were all suspended from school. For a few days Raheem could not tell his mom that she had warned him about had happened. He began to think that school was going to be a wrap. Raheem did not know how to deliver the news. About two weeks later they got a letter from Irvington Municipal Court. They were charging him with simple battery. The document mentioned the possibility of receiving eighteen months in the state youth house. When they attended court the first time, Johnny's people did not show up, but the charges weren't dropped. Another date was set. Raheem could not go back to school until he was seen at court. A month went by before he returned to Irvington Tech.

At the second court date, it was discovered that Raheem's grandmother and Johnny's grandmother were affiliated by way of a church organization. Raheem was unaware that his grandmother had a little bit of money. His mom had no money. His thinking was if Mom had to foot the bill for any of this mess, he would have to do the entire eighteen months. She didn't have it; this was extra, and he would have to do what he had to do. No bailout for him. God saw fit to intervene in this seemingly impossible situation. Somehow the two grandmothers came to an agreement that Johnny's medical bills would be paid. The charges were dropped. Some papers were signed, the judge dropped his gavel, and the matter came to a close. It was one of the most important days in the history of Raheem's life. He unequivocally understood God's favor and made a conscious decision to live a life that showed his great appreciation for his second chance.

The Newark boxing elite who came out of gyms like Eighth Street and the Dukist AC boxing clubs were some of the first to comprehend the new youngster. Martial arts were growing, blossoming into something quite special. New York, Philadelphia, Connecticut,

Maryland and other cities were witnessing similar experiences. Newark was still considered to be a boxing town, but martial arts would continue chipping away at that title.

No one ever considered Newark a large city. Many of the first-generation students, who belonged to a multitude of martial art schools, were very skilled and quite good. Its population was not large, but it was rather explosive with raw and natural talent. In the late 1960s through the late 1970s Newark was a dominating powerhouse in the Northeast United States. No other city or town of its size produced such numbers of highly skilled martial artists.

The *Five Fingers of Death* was playing at every local movie theater. You might ask, "What's the big deal?" It was the great film classic that started everything off.

Young people who were participating in the sport already knew the true beauty of the art form. The rest of the world was being served with papers to wake up and start to fall in love. Like nothing that they had ever seen before, folks were mesmerized. A typical martial artist could now say to regular people, "This is what I do." For people who were used to being bullied, hope was now knocking at their doors. Raheem and others saw immediate increases in class enrollment. Kids told their parents, "Mom, Dad, that karate stuff we saw at the movies—that's what I want to learn." In three or four weeks, another karate movie was released. The Asian film producers saw a pot of gold at the end of the rainbow. They took full advantage of the opportunity.

Back in the day, there wasn't any protective equipment at all. A few people were smart enough to put in a mouth piece. Your knuckles were wrapped, and you just fought.

In one match Raheem went up against a gentlemen name Kevin "Sleepy" Friday. The match was very sloppy and uninspiring. Raheem won the decision, but he didn't feel it was a win. His family was there, and he was truly embarrassed by that fiasco.

Fate writes the script that you don't know about yet. At a martial arts event Raheem participated in, he would experience his first and only defeat. His opponent was a gifted student named Osbourne Shabazz. His sensei was Grand Master James Fame. It was a full contact match. Osbourne Shabazz brought his A game to the outing and managed to dominate Raheem. To this very day Raheem does not hold back, saying, "That brother put some sport on me!" That loss wasn't the end of the world to Raheem, was not a derailment. It came at the right time in his martial arts career. He did not have an egocentric attitude, so it was a teachable moment.

He traveled in New York to the Sunny Side Dojo. Master Ron Van Clief gave Raheem a lift home every now and then on rainy days, every once in a while, his sensei made an unexpected visit. Sometimes Raheem wondered about the difference between teacher/student and friend-to-friend relationships. Attending a new school, students must start over as a while belt, regardless of their skills. When Raheem had earned his purple belt, something happened that made it impossible to have money for karate class. Master Ron Van Clief came by to see what was up with Raheem. The situation was explained to him, and he welcomed Raheem back to class, with the understanding that payment would not be an issue. He told Raheem to return and stay with the journey. From purple belt to black belt, there was no money involved.

Bruce Lee is back in the arena. Everyone's buddy comes back on the scene in a huge and crazy way in a movie called *Fist of Fury*. People anywhere on the planet, who saw his movie simply lost their minds. Planet Earth was relatively quiet until the release of *Fist of Fury*.

Every new release of a karate movie passed the current movie on the big screen. Bruce Lee brought martial arts to Main Street, USA, approximately every six months or so he delivered a new movie. People loved him, and the relationship deepened a little more with each new movie.

No longer just a boxing town, Newark was now officially a martial arts town! It didn't make any difference where you were, kids all over the place were jumping and doing flying kicks. Some large events might be held in a large gymnasium where multiple karate schools were using the space together. Young men and a few young ladies began competing against one another, honing their skills. A few began to distinguish themselves with their excellent kicking abilities. Every time there was some type of outing, eyes searched. Nearly every person on hand was conducting a mental scouting report. Raheem was developing a reputation for being a leg technician. A visionary by the name of Mike Goodwin gave Raheem the nickname "Lizard." He was slender and terribly quick. He became known as Raheem "The Lizard" Gardner." Often a nickname was more recognized than a real name: Little KA, the Eighth Wonder of the World, Mr. Graceful, Happy Robot Crump, Rubberband Man, Darrell the Technician were some of the nicknames that publicly announced their owner's intention to woo you or knock you out.

Grand Master Ron Van Clief set Raheem up in an eight-hundred-square-foot satellite karate school. It was located on North Munn and South Orange Avenue, across the street from Churches Chicken and the bus stop. A set of keys was handed to him. His confidence in Raheem was greater than what Raheem himself believed. One early evening he was teaching class at the dojo, working with some of the students. He was responsible for training thirteen students in the fine Asian tradition. All of a sudden, a gang of martial artists burst into the school. Everything went from calm to total chaos in a matter of mere seconds. Raheem and all the students in the building were under serious attack. Feverish kicks and punches came to their faces, heads, and bodies. These fighters came in the door with the sole intention of taking them out, as if in a bad karate movie. Raheem was only a red belt on the evening of that brazen attack. It was a bad situation. Basically all they could do was try to protect themselves from the punishment and the multiple whippings being administered. It lasted two minutes or so, but it seemed like a lifetime. Surprisingly enough, this kind of savage behavior was not uncommon. Riffraff could be found in many schools.

In the early 1970s, a fast-growing martial arts chain school exploded from out of nowhere. A few businessmen were taking things to the next level. They understood the future business model and knew how to run a school. Their franchise operated between New York and New Jersey, where they opened a record number of schools. The head instructors were commercially promoted to expedite quick expansion. Some schools had a different vision for their future. They repeatedly kicked in dojo doors, beat up the instructors, and told them to close up shop.

Martial arts schools all over the world basically teach peacefulness, harmony, hard work, and self-discipline. Many things can start off a certain way, but not many remain pure. In Asia, martial arts are not viewed as a sport but as a way of life.

Grand Master James Chectim lost his life in a terrible airplane tragedy. To his credit, he trained some fine and outstanding students. In his martial arts clan a few local legends arose. Some of the leadership did continue to refine the skills of our Asian brothers. Harmonious coexistence did not prove to be deeply rooted in the dojo of the not-so-distant past. Slowly darker energy pressed toward the forefront. A glass of water was knocked over on a kitchen table, and things began to get messy. A few instructors carried on with the ways that were taught to them. An arrogant and boastful mindset appeared. One sensei and a few students tried to duplicate their own version of Muhammad Ali. The genie was let out of the bottle. From that point on, no one was going to be comfortable in a martial arts setting.

Newcomers, take notice. Your defensive blocks will definitely need to be on point to ensure you will not need to pick up your teeth and choose a new hobby. If you are fortunate enough to learn these concepts early, your face and body will appreciate it.

Grand Master Ron Van Clief was off in Japan and California making movies. Grand Master Moses Powell and Master Amastah Watson took on the duties of running the school. They were also in charge of all the teaching that would take place. In his absence they were the primary teachers of Chinese Go Shu. For his four months away and the four months back at school, this cycle was continuous. For the entire time Raheem was attending the Sunny Side Dojo, this was the norm. These men were like father figures, influencing student life. Not only were they good people, they also happened to be among the most respected martial artists on the East Coast.

You're on a bus and then a train to New York City to attend your instructor's dojo. Things begin to get a little crazy. The weekend has come, and it's time to see a movie—but not just any movie. This one happens to be one of the many movies that your sensei has made and is starring in. You know now that you are in a special place. Not just any school. The sensei has tapped into something much bigger than New Jersey or New York. Extending far, reaching outside of the United States, this satisfying expression is massive. Your friends and you are downtown Newark at the Paramount theater. It is outrageous. You're at the dojo next to your sensei, and four months later the world is seeing the fruits of his labor. You are so proud, and you want everybody in the movie theater to know, "Hey, that's my instructor!" but each time you and your classmates see your sensei on the big screen, it feels surreal. The final thought is, They have no idea*!*

Percolating in the city of Newark, New Jersey, in the late 1960s through the mid-1970s, a city not considered large in anyone's imagination, with a population of a few hundred thousand people, something very special was in effect. In a multitude of martial arts schools, first-generation students were more than just good or average. Raw and explosive talent began to illuminate from within the ranks, young people like Mr. Graceful, Happy Robot Crump, Eugene Floyd, Reginald Goode, Darryl Technician, Jesse Harris, T. Little Roker, Troy Norman, Master G. Rubberband Man, Kason, Lee Roy Huggins, and Little kA. There were many more up-and-coming hopefuls helping to elevate Newark's competitive landscape. No other town or city of its size in the United States was turning out such gifted martial artists. To be good or okay was unacceptable thinking they could not embrace. They woke up in the morning believing in their hearts and souls that they would rise above and beyond everyone else. "All of these jokers are doing their thing, and when the dust settles I will be the one standing on top of the mountain."

Raheem participated in many karate tournaments in the Tri-State area. Weapons, forms, brick breaking, sparring, and full contact, Basically, if something was going on, he was right there in the thick of it. His contemporaries were raw, fierce, and highly motivated to build a reputation by beating him up and embarrassing him.

A martial artist by the name of Earl Ross actively produced local and out-of-state events between 1974 and 1977. These tournaments took place at the Civic Center in North Philly and Raheem participated in the hardcore tournaments. In the first two years he could sense the Philly competitors didn't appreciate the success of the Jersey artists. Driving his own car, Raheem would bring four others with him to the anarchy. Outside of the contest rings, fights took place later in the parking lot. The trophies were placed on the ground near the car for the real fisticuffs going on. The trophies were then hurried into the car, and they made a quick getaway. On the highway going back home they understood that high drama was not confined to Newark, New Jersey.

The unpredictability of what he would see on a week to week basis was mind numbing. Some schools had disciplined students who held up fine martial arts traditions. On the other hand, some brought plenty of drama to the mix. The competition he faced left an indelible stamp on Raheem's psyche. During that era, a lot of young people didn't know much about such things as schizophrenia. Many years later the term *bipolar* would better describe the behavior of a few on that path. You could say there was never a dull moment at any event. Things were lively and always interesting, to say that the least. Referees would call for a hold in the action, and many late punches or kicks would still land. A number of students were regularly disqualified during sparring competitions. The judges themselves were not off limits and were harassed at many events. When it came to schools with weak foundations and unqualified instructors, the intimidation factor was critical. Week after week such dishonorable behavior was an ordinary occurrence. In many communities around the country Little Johnny attended a local martial arts affair and not much went off script. Not so in Raheem's neck of the woods. A large number of lives were affected. Anyone who attended the outings on a regular basis endured physiological flogging on a subliminal level. Sensitive persons who tended to be low key took the biggest hit of all. Nice, quiet folk were pushed out of the boat. If a person saw martial arts as a hobby or was casual practitioners, there simply wasn't a place for them. The culture

CHAPTER 3

Before he knew it, four years had rolled by and graduation day was upon him. It was clearly time to move on. In September 1977, Raheem received his long-awaited black belt from Grand Master Ron Von Clief. A product of two schools, Raheem had spent many long hours of hard work and dedication. Master Bozc, cofounder of the Turtle System, and Grand Master Ron Von Clief did a great job of preparing him thoroughly.

A new member of the United States Army, Raheem traveled to El Paso, Texas, in October 1977. Basic training wasn't a physical challenge to him because of his many years of martial arts training. In those few short weeks, he would witness some of the recruits transform from being overweight to lean and trim. The culture shock was having drill instructors in his face and calling him everything but a child of God. One inch away, face to face, that's how they did it in the military. As a civilian, parents may have tended to baby men about their responsibilities. In the US Army, that didn't happen! They tore recruits down to let them know that it's not all about them. In no uncertain terms, they let them know that they would conform to their wishes. They'd jump however high they told them to and reply, "Sir, yes sir." People downplay the confrontational style that the army utilizes to get attention. Let no one fool you; the average person will need several weeks to adjust to the military outlook of an individual's overall importance. When they signed those papers, it changed things. "You will do what we tell you, how we tell you, and when we tell you. Is that *understood*? Boy, I can't hear you—*speak up!*"

In El Paso, Texas, he met Grand Master Charles Dixon, founder of Shaolin Goju. President and CEO of Shinjimasu International Martial Arts Association, Raheem was on holdover status, only twelve weeks removed from Newark. He was given orders that sent him to the beautiful islands of Hawaii. There he would become a member of the 8th Army Karate Team. The all-Army Tae-Kwan-Do Karate team would provide Raheem with a lot of support, discipline, and structure. Room and board was free, and he received a paycheck twice a month. For five years, from the age of nineteen to twenty-four years old, he was away from home, doing what he'd been connected to for half of his life. When he first got there he was pretty raw about executing his techniques. He realized that he had to slow down a bit on the violence. He had left Newark, but his mindset was still urban. A maturing process began. Back home in

New Jersey, everything was all about self-defense: protect yourself; do what you have to do.

Landing on the airstrip in Hawaii, on a time-treasured piece of real estate that people all over the world often fantasized about, was an experience that he would never forget. The fresh, colorful, fruity flowers and strong pineapple scent in the air were heavenly. It took a few weeks for his nose to normalize the pleasant odor. Extremely beautiful women welcomed him with leis placed around his neck. He pinched himself to see whether or not he was dreaming. When he woke up the next day, nothing had changed, so he knew that it was all real.

Although Raheem did not experience any problems on the Hawaiian Islands, it was still necessary to obtain knowledge of the local area. Anywhere a person travels, there is an undercurrent. The army, air force, and navy were all pretty cool, but a small number of marines made things a little rough from time to time. In the eyes of a young Samoan growing up on the island, knowing the beautiful ladies, tourism was a big deal in those parts. A young ego-maniac marine feels like he's the most invincible thing walking the planet. The thought process might be, "When off duty I will drink as much as I please. If I see a woman who catches my eye I will have my way with respect or by force, however it comes." A native islander doesn't feel or tolerate that. His thinking is, *My homeland, my long-time companions. It isn't happening. Drunk or not, marine or whomever, our women will be respected.* Every now and then Raheem might hear about a soldier who was found dead in a pineapple field.

Now away from New Jersey and New York, he could begin to see how vast and wide the influence of this remarkable Asian expression was. The thoughts of self-defense would have to be put on a shelf. He would take a different look at it as a sport and possible business. His thinking became, *Can I actually make money doing what I love?*

He could see the possibilities for teaching martial arts to become extremely marketable. *Can I offer this information to help protect others, not only to protect myself?* The raw element that caused him to flourish would have to be modified a bit. He could take things to a whole other level by adding intelligent thought to the training process. Then the total experience could be enhanced. Hawaii became the steppingstone that helped him grow as a man. There was still something missing inside of him. One year earlier a little brother was born into the Gardner family. Most of his support came from his grandmother, Mom, and two sisters. For many years people had been telling Raheem that he was pretty good. A father or uncle wasn't on hand to help him connect the dots. It would take a while, but he would have to figure some things out for himself.

When he started competing in international competitions, the wins kept coming. Hardly any different from when he was in Newark, the wins came with a sense of fear. Some of his teammates won also, but they had a boatload of confidence. The eye of the tiger had eluded him for many years before a light bulb came on and he finally got it! *I guess I am good at this.* The confidence component seemed to make a big difference from that point onward.

After a little while the confidence took a turn and become arrogance. Ego had seized him for a minute after hearing a few comments, and he knew that his case of big-head had to be reeled in. He returned to his regular self, with confidence at a healthy level. In Honolulu, Hawaii, he won first place in karate tournaments over and over until 1981. He competed in more than sixty tournaments all over the island. Under the guidance of Grand Master Charles Dixon, he competed and won all over the world. He became a member of Shinjimasu International Association in March of 1981. In this organization he also taught martial arts as a black belt.

People stood closely around him, communicating with this soft-spoken, quiet soul. Eyes made contact, but some still failed to see his underlying concern. For a number of years he would get by, not fully satisfied with an important part of his life. The maturation process of his martial arts world seemed to be clicking quite well. He was truthful within himself from early on. Karate was very satisfying on a number of levels, but it could not be the end-all that life had to offer. The developmental stage of Raheems educational experience was not up to par. It may not have been on the surface of many of his conversations, but the persistent reminder was always at the front of his conscious. Because his world was still growing and expanding, he came to know that those portions of his life could get better.

From the back of his mind to the very forefront, it was clear that time was now. He decided that things had to turn around. Looking to the very near future, he made a commitment that when time became available he would better himself. His vision was to blend two worlds into one. His past experiences could use an educational enhancement to facilitate his very own signature training.

In his travels around the world he passed through places like Panama, Hong Kong, and Korea. He spent a short time at Fort Stewart, Georgia. There he competed and became the 124-pound world karate champion.

The conversation started about him teaching others the art of tect kung chi goju, Shaolin goju karate. In August 1982 he was located in Osterholz Schoranbeck, Germany. He went through Bremarhaven, Germany. The army base and airfield was located in northwest Germany, east of London, England, and west of Denmark. Bremerhaven was a transshipment hub, the sixteenth largest port in the world, serving the waterways of the North Sea and the North Atlantic Ocean. His tour in Germany lasted from 1983 to 1987. It became his first opportunity to operate his own karate school. He was the first student in Shinjimasu International Martial Arts Association to become an international instructor. The school was filled to capacity by more than one hundred students, military personnel, a lieutenant colonel, a major, a captain, and family members and their teenagers.

Raheem learned how to generate business proposals, stating his mission, goals, and results that would be achieved. An E-5 active duty soldier during the day, he headed a full-blown school in the evenings, teaching six days a week. With his salary, the school afforded him the ability to purchase a brand-new BMW. His military pay did not allow such a purchase. Every dime he earned was one hundred percent profit. The school was called North Dutch Land Youth Lands Activity Center. There was no overhead. Everything was provided: van, gas card, protective equipment and gear. The school was a little more upscale, and he added educational value to the delivery. He charged sixty-five dollars a month. Financially, he was in a good place.

To become a martial arts master required knowing at least two or three disciplines. The importance of broadening one's martial arts education was essential. When he moved to New Haven, Connecticut, later, he left his organization and began to learn a different style. Raheem began to learn Tang Soo Doo Muk Do Kwan at the New Haven Martial Arts Academy in Guilford, Connecticut. Already a fourth-degree black belt, he moved from white belt to black belt in thirteen months. In the next twelve months, he progressed from black belt to third-degree black belt. This achievement addressed the Korean aspect he needed to add to his arts repertoire. His base now covered Okinawan, Chinese, and Korean styles.

For a brief time he trained in Korea with the Rock Soldiers. The highlight of the training was award ceremony day. The hardcore combat training meant the soldiers received patches for their uniforms that honored their level of achievement. Raheem had not seen this anywhere else, and he thought that it was fascinating.

After Germany, Raheem had the opportunity to live and grow his martial arts experience in places like Texas, North Carolina, South Carolina, and Georgia. Between 1991 and 1992 he visited Korea for the second time in his travels.

Just a bit past the age of thirty, Raheem experienced an important juncture. The All-Army 8th Karate Team had him traveling the world many times over. He heard a lot of great speeches and many promises that were not even close to being kept. For a solid twenty years he had made it his sole choice to be a Muslim. His mom did not oppose to his changing to Islam. His grandmother was a praying woman of Christian belief. He would say that she often prayed for him, even when he wasn't praying for himself. But no airplane was ever purchased for Muhammad, and a hospital was never built. Being true to himself with all that he had observed about the Christian faith, he began to establish a relationship with Christ. For some time he was very much aware of the favor that Christ had bestowed upon him. Everywhere in the world his feet made contact with ground, he experienced success. He knew that it had nothing to do with luck. Luck and Newark, New Jersey, did not share a common denominator. It took a lot of hard work and effort to become a local legend. People who influenced him and instructors and trainers had to be spot on. In the international arena, he made it a habit of winning for the twelve years that he was on the karate team. The competition he faced came from all over the world. Handlers of some boxers or martial artists craft a career that may not be as solid as their records appeared to be. This luxury to build a shallow but impressive set of stats never existed for him.

The old saying had much truth to it: What doesn't kill you will make you stronger! His hardest and strongest competitions took place in

Newark, New Jersey. In the early days he normally didn't display the greatest amount of self-reliance in a sparring match, but you could not find anyone who had more heart. Those who weathered the urban storms generally leaned toward a balance of fearlessness. In situations where a normal person would be scared to death, the inner self kicked in and said, "We don't have time for nonsense." From the mid-1970s to the present day, he placed first or second in forms, weapons, and breaking competitions. In sparring contests in that time frame he experienced no losses.

After more than a twenty-year military career, Raheem was now free to do as he saw fit. The past had been good to him, but now he could live his life on his own terms. You could say that he had some positive hits. He could argue that some things were amiss because of the military landscape, with all its uncertainties. Full control was never really in his hands. He'd been in some trenches and through trials and tribulations. He'd lived in some places he really didn't care for and worked at times for some difficult and impulsive people. The Columbus Karate Academy would be his first school as a civilian. In 1993, he said. "I will buy some houses, open up a school, and see where it takes me." Two years later he opened to the ideal of training small children. His mind had to be cleared of some harsh things he'd witnessed as a youngster coming up in the martial arts world. When his mind was purged, he was ready to receive students of any age. Enrollment was about thirty-five students. The school was doing decent business.

The battle of Atlanta was an unexpected turning point for the school. It would be responsible for transforming a respectable but ordinary school to one of national and international prominence. All of the children of the school participated in an extremely professionally staged tournament, with about seven thousand eight hundred people in attendance.. Three of his sons had first-place finishes. Even with the large number of schools in attendance, it was Columbus Karate Academy's day. One of the event's organizers, Mr. Joe Proley, and film star and world-renowned grand master Superfoot Bill Wallace paid a good deal of attention to Raheem's five-year-old son. They asked, "Who taught this five-year-old these long, intricate sequences to remember and execute?" In the martial arts world, everyone's heard of Superfoot Bill Wallace. At this event he and Dr. Gardner met for the first time. He asked Dr. Gardner if he would be interested in representing the state of Georgia on ESPN's Wide World of Sports. The event was shown on television about five times, and school enrollment went through the roof. From all over the country they came, from New Jersey, New York, Philly, Detroit, DC, and Miami. From that day forward his school would not be looked upon the same.

CHAPTER 4

The 2007 stock market crash came down like a great tsunami. The rich got richer, and everybody else received a much smaller slice of the great American pie. Translation to English; African Americans, Hispanics, and all other minorities had the long end of the stick shoved a little farther up their backsides. Not since the Great Depression had so many Caucasians felt that same cold stick thrust up their backsides. Things became difficult, with a lot of uncertainty in the air.

In the closet, or in the open, a terrible day in the history of the Ku Klux Klan came. On the other hand, people of color were completely exuberant! A healthy number of Caucasians were also enthusiastic about the first African American president elected in US history. Only a small number of people on the planet could have imagined this taken place. The 2008 presidential jubilation was short lived. The African American community and worldwide onlookers did a double take to believe what they had just witnessed. Millions of so-called God fearing people of various religious practices felt all too comfortable about disrespecting President Barack Obama. African Americans who were fifty years of age or older had no public or private reason to be shocked. The pile of *dung* that he inherited had a stench that could probably be smelled all the way on the surface of the moon. The previous president hadn't experienced any opposition for a period of six years.

The community outreach program wasn't expanding on its own. Like Parks and Recreations, Columbus Community Center, and Girls, Inc., they had a captive audience, and they wanted him to add a martial arts component to what they were doing. The children in the United States are some of the most obsessed in the world. His degree in fitness and nutrition meshed well with what was needed for the children. He promised to keep the prices really, really low. In most such programs, the parents couldn't afford to pay for their children. A lot of parents were economically challenged. The parents paid for the various community-based programs, and they in turn paid him. No money came directly through the parents.

Over the past years, Dr. Raheem Gardner had won many awards and trophies at some meaningful and memorable events. On November 29, 2010, Dr. Raheem Gardner, CEO, was named Male Role Model of the Year. He was also the recipient of a certificate of Special Congressional Recognition from US Congressman Sanford D. Bishop, Jr. Raheem had no idea he was in the running for the award. A woman named Carol Birdy had called Dr. Gardner to inform him that he should attend an important function at Ebony Baptist Church. Several gentlemen were nominated, and he was the winner. Not a single thing connected to that evening had shown up on his radar. He was completely in the dark about the recognition and presentation of the award. He was in a state of shock, which he welcomed with open arms. Afterwards he would say to Ms. Carol, "Did you know about all of this?" She said yes! Ms. Carol and the community held discussions about the various candidates and his name kept emerging with much enthusiasm. The opportunity for him to promote himself never came into play. This award would bring confirmation that trust and great expectation from his character were well placed. Of all his martial arts accomplishments, this award was the pinnacle of his life.

No head of state with a sophisticated army wakes up one morning and says, "Give me the Yellow Pages." To have a qualified martial arts master came in and train your soldiers in hand-to-hand combat is no light matter. Being highly skilled alone would not bring you into the conversation.

A highly decorated colonel hands some folders to the motivated and optimistic general. He and his staff have been considering prospects for some time. Extensive professional and personal background checks are done. Character comes into play as strongly as unique skill sets. "Colonel, what else do we know about Master Raheem Gardner? His pedigree is all about winning. One of his top students is a military contractor doing some work in Dubai. According to the recommendation of his student and our background research, this might be the right fit for our needs."

"Colonel, contact Dr. Gardner. Let's bring some closure to this matter."

"Okay, General, consider it done."

In the immediate area other candidates include Egyptians and Africans. Their short list could easily include individuals representing the four corners of the earth. With the enormous international paperwork load, the process to get the licensing to teach males would take about two years. The satellite school was in its third year.

Since he was a little boy, he'd stuck with his art and was able to reach the highest level of achievement. Pause for a minute and really think about it. It's like being in elementary school and moving up to the twelfth grade and then going on to receive an associate's, bachelor's, master's, and then a doctorate degree, he majored in fitness and a minored in nutrition. Things learned in Newark, New Jersey, that he had been doing since way back when, incorporating many of those things into his everyday life, working for himself and being happy. "Man, we need to write a book!"

Human beings always want to know they fit into the big picture. Many life markers help us to gage the time invested and poured into the depth of our souls. He had done martial arts nearly all of his life. A master ranking in this lifestyle was very fulfilling. The punches, kicks, blocks, spins, leaps, and breath control became visible evidence of his expression. Along the sometimes-lonely journey he saw a lot of growth. Raheem could no longer do martial arts because it was now who he was. Every fiber in his body and mind was set in this ancient polished treasure. A call was put out to move on to the next chapter in martial arts. His mentor, an extraordinary individual, was called upon: Grand Master Jackie Cotton. This gentleman had no choice about his involvement in this lifestyle. At the age of three his father decided that it was the way he would go. Fifteen-plus years ago, they had met in Little Rock, Arkansas, at a function for their karate association.

Grand Master Cotton and Master Gardner were part of the same organization since the late 1970s. Gardner represented the southern region of the United States. Grand Master Cotton represented the western region of the United States. An ex-member of the United States Special Forces, Brother Cotton was a member of the Navy's martial arts karate team. On that team, he enjoyed a good deal of success and competed in many places all over the world, such as Japan, Korea, Thailand, Hong Kong, the Philippines, Singapore, Australia, and Africa. In March 2011, he came to Columbus Karate Academy to perform the tenth degree black belt promotion for grand masters. A lot of years, sweat, blood, perseverance, and grind had come to a defining head. This celebration took place at the headquarters' expanded facility at 1107 Henry Avenue in the city of Columbus, Georgia.

There were other satellite schools, but the main school at 1107 Henry Avenue was a place you always remembered. The dojo is always immaculate. Dr. Gardner was his momma's son, a clean freak. When you first enter the building and if you happened to be blind, you would swear it was a botanical garden you were in. The place was clean and disinfected, but the aroma would blow you away. Your nose would simply say to you, "Wow!"

We had reached some lows in the free era since slavery, bottom-of-the-pit lows. In 2013/2014, self-respect and social etiquette were almost nonexistent. Female-to-female and male-to-female daily interactions were disrespectful. Lowdown derogatory female names were the common vernacular that caused hardly anyone to raise an eyebrow. The good news was that back in Raheem's day, the young men had a sense of class and a great deal of respect for young ladies. If we could look at a social date from the past, this was how it was done back in the mid-1970s.

Raheem is on Bergen Street on the corner of Lyon's Avenue. Across the street he sees a beautiful sister, but he realizes that she is much more than that. She is fine, a classification that should not be used lightly. (Don't use this word unless you are looking at beauty at its apex.) He makes his way over to the other side of the street and is about three feet behind her. He thinks, *I have to rap to this ebony princess. If I don't, someone else is likely to do so soon.*

"Excuse me, miss." The young lady turns around. She looks surprised, but she answers, "Yes?"

"My name is Raheem. Are looking for an address?"

"Well, yes and no."

"Can I get past your beauty and ask your name?"

"Yes, you can. My name is Karen."

"What high school do you attend?"

"I go to Central High. What school do you go to, Raheem?"

"I go to Irvington Tech. Everyone isn't going to go to college, so it's a school where you can learn a trade."

"I'm looking for Mapes Avenue."

"Oh, that's just two blocks away."

"My aunt lives there, and I'm on my way to her house."

"Would you feel comfortable if I walk with you to her house?"

"I would be okay with that."

"Is there a man in your life?"

"Wow! You don't waste time. The answer is no. How about you? Do you have a girlfriend?"

"Right now I'm single. Karen, what are you doing this weekend?"

"No plans yet."

"How about seeing a movie?"

"I went to see a movie last weekend."

"Do you skate?"

"Yes."

"Can I pick you up Saturday at seven?"

"Yes, but how will we be traveling?"

"I have an old black car. It's no Cadillac, but it runs and it's mine. Twin City Roller Rink, Saturday at seven."

"Yes, I'd like that."

"Karen, can you skate?"

"You'll find out soon enough."

"I'll need your telephone number to make this all good."

"Nice meeting you, Raheem."

"Karen, enjoy your visit with your aunt. I'll call you later. Oh, one more thing. What's the latest time I can call you?"

"Before ten. After ten, my father will have some choice words for you."

"I can respect that. Talk to you later."

Many people get up every day to go to work, and they hate everybody at the job, including the boss. Raheem gets up every day, eager to get to work. Many of the things that he has experienced he could not have planned. God gets all the credit for how his life came together. If he had tried to plan it, it would never have worked out. Married for more than twenty-eight years, he has five children and nine grandchildren. His children are successful in their endeavors; no one is in jail or on drugs or in rehabilitation, which is quite a blessing. A good family name was already in place, starting with his grandmother and mother. His living was built on the solid foundation that served as a family heritage statement. If your last name was Gardner, failure was not an option. You were not required to be the smartest in the room, but you were expected to try your best at whatever you did, definitely not always at this level.

Out of Newark, New Jersey, came some of the most talented and hardest-working people the world has ever come to know. Unfortunately, young people never heard these things said about their city. God being who He is blesses whom He chooses in ways that affect many lives to be. Martial arts became the answer to a nagging question, "How am I going to protect me and my two little sisters?" With hard work and dedication, the answer would extend far beyond that of his family alone. Dr. Gardner would become responsible for helping thousands of individuals from around the world gain a sense of personal safety.

One of Raheem's goals was to be able to qualify for and compete in Olympic competition. It would be a great honor to represent his country and meet some of the world's elite competitors. Although he did Japanese karate, his organization was associated with Korean-style Tae Kwan Do martial arts. It didn't matter how great a martial artist he was, not being part of certain organizations would not allow him in the door. Through USA Kick, he was able to qualify for and win his first Olympic gold medal in 1999. He went on to win other medals in 2002, 2004, and 2006. Raheem was blessed from the start with world-class masters and grand masters who prepared him well. Newark's native son's explosive and unpredictable encounters pushed him to succeed and pass any test put before him. Although he did not participate himself, he sent a team to the Olympics in 2008 and 2010.

Moving through the world, it became necessary to begin keeping a mental file to try to decide where he might one day live and settle down, drop that anchor, and get on with his personal agenda. The state of Georgia topped the last of the many places he might possibly settle. The people were nice and friendly. Raheem could visualize a life vastly different from what he'd experienced in his early days. If he felt a need for an intense nightlife, the city of Atlanta was nearby. The number of suburban communities also helped to tip the scales.

Having been around the block a few times, we kind of accept the fact that very few will leave this earth in perfect health. It's been said that twenty-five to thirty years of age is the peak of physical life. From that point on, it's assumed that it's all downhill. More than a decade ago, Dr. Gardner discovered that he had inherited some health issues: diabetes, high blood pressure, high cholesterol, and glaucoma. Having medical coverage and good doctors, Raheem has been able to maintain his health in relatively good condition. His physical fitness regimen combined with his nutritional knowledge made it possible to continue and progress. With all that is going on, his level of martial arts execution is still at a very high level. He looks forward to doing what he does for a very long time.

Opening the doors of the dojo, he can feel the deep history that runs through Columbus Karate Academy, housed in the same building for more than twenty years. Some of the original children are nearly thirty years of age. He is now training and instructing children of the children he came to know. Masters and grand masters who have been around for a long time can truly identify with this situation, seeing little ones come through the doors for the very first time, nurturing them along, watching them grow up before your very eyes, and then entrusting their little ones to you also. It brings a smile to his face and heart at the same time.

In the midst of a terrible worldwide recession, Dr. Gardner had the main school in Columbus, Georgia, and three other satellite locations. Untold numbers of big businesses and huge corporations went under in the United States and many other places in the world.

Some people went back home to their countries because they could not find work. Organizations he trained for included the Columbus Police Department, Buena Vista Police Department, Columbus Sheriff Department, Columbus Homeland Security, Parks and Recreation, and Girls, Inc. He kept his bids low for the professional police organizations and was not money driven. He was able to provide them with training that was detailed and comprehensive. Parks and Recreations, Girls, Inc., and after-school programs hired him to provide martial arts instructions for their programs. He did not receive money from the parents of the children. The money came through the city or towns that sponsored the programs. Sometimes they were a month behind, but they would always do right by him. The United States had some of the most obese children in the world, and his fitness and nutritional backgrounds were a big plus in those programs.

For the next four years God got all of the credit for the expansion he experienced. Dr. Gardner lived right to the best of his abilities and kept his faith strong. In a four-year period he had the main school and seven other satellite locations. One of the schools was in Kuwait; his top student, who was instrumental in setting up the Kuwait school, instructed in that part of the world. The other locations were instructed by his wife, a son who was driving at that time, a secretary, and students. Raheem headed two locations. The country was experiencing devastation. In that period a number of martial arts schools fell by the wayside, and he was being blessed with expansion.

The invisible hand of greatness will never visit a person or place and request to be a part of a popularity poll. It's bigger than what people think or feel. Before he walked through a door his name was much more important than anyone could imagine. More than only the state of Georgia, the Southern martial arts region appreciated this man. With time comes understanding that expectations are always connected to your name. Tell a group of people that Dr. Gardner will be in the room and the energy level will rise to a high level.

Raheem reached the age of fifty-six in 2013. That year he engaged in sparring competitions a total of three times. Win or lose, it was not time to rest on his past performances or personal records. Destiny would have to reveal to him where he now stood in relation to his lifelong journey. When you begin to climb in age there are no lies to embrace. Either you still have it or your best days are behind you. In somewhere between three and four hundred victories since the mid-1970s the outcome were favorable.

Many of the earlier karate movies had a central theme or message, which was "We have the best martial arts school." It was definitely a special time in the evolution of self-defense and fighting art forms. In the modern era things were much different. Students were a great deal calmer and more reserved in their outward expressions during competition. Dr. Gardner's students were very confident, but they didn't brag about how good they were.

In the spring of 2014, Dr. Gardner arrived at a southern regional tournament in Florida, a good-sized event with a wide range of martial arts disciplines represented. He went with fourteen students, who brought along their parents to provide the love and support all participants appreciated. It was a Friday night; the contest was a two-day event. They hired a wing of a hotel and had a great time. Not a single person was smoking, drinking, or getting high. They simply enjoyed the evening before the competition started. Saturday morning, just after breakfast, a rules meeting was held to discuss what was available and how the referees were judging. Columbus Karate Academy always expected to do well at any type of meet they attended. Three out of five first-place trophies brought joy to the heart of any grand master. In the two days of competition the school earned eleven first-place finishes and three third-place finishes. For

Dr. Gardner to garner so much success over four decades was truly remarkable. His students knew his rich martial arts history and pursued excellence following his lead. The same techniques and principles that placed Dr. Gardner where he was also launched his students to success. Two generations behind him were learning the same things that he had at ten years old. His heart was overjoyed at being a part of those young lives.

All good managers keep an eye toward the future. Personnel had to be prepared to assume responsibilities, and a trust factor must be built up. Dr. Gardner addressed the issues with a flexible future timetable between five to seven years. No one lives forever; that is universal to everyone and everything. Someone would have to fill his shoes. As long as the torch still burned, he planned to keep in shape as best he could while he transitioned to an administrative mode. Even then he would offer private instruction to the black belts, giving them the right information so that they did things the correct way. When he was not present, he wanted them to operate as if he were standing right there. Errors had to be corrected so that the art was perfected, no different than if he were performing himself.

Special treatment was not afforded to Dr. Gardner, even in the midst of such an amazing life. The fallout after the presidential election proved to be a quandary of grand distinction. Many who were legally able to cast a vote stumbled over something that was already known. The United States was close to being split right down the middle of its social fabric. The slight majority belonged to the genuinely positive people of the nation. These people wanted the world to see the United States at our very best. Jaw-dropping and eye-opening things just kept coming into the mix. A number of presidential security breaches happened. Since the time of John F. Kennedy, there hadn't seemed to be any such problems. Outside of the African American members of society, the rest of the citizens didn't seem to get it. Skepticism and subplots of treachery loomed over the heads of those labeled as minorities. Once again, a good number of political, as well as religious, leaders of many different faiths let the people down. Their commitment was firmly about lining their own pockets.

Another champion of human and civil rights lent his voice of support to the commander in chief, our thirty-ninth president, Jimmy Carter. He came out strongly and denounced the political tactics of the other party. His courage and backbone gave him the moral authority to call it was it was, pure and simple—racism. Not a single soul stood by his side. He was on an island by himself. The economy was allowed to sputter along.

For the first time in modern history, medical coverage became affordable for a larger number of people. Basically, more people could live for significantly longer. Vice President Joseph Biden said, "This is a big deal."

Osama Bin Laden was cornered and killed. No one saw that coming. President Barack Obama was smart enough to trust so few. You can almost hear Michelle whispering to her husband late at night, "Honey, keep your circle small and tight." We saw that the world did not end. The recovery of the economy was steady, slow, and painful.

Raheem was living a steady regimen of martial arts, day in and day out—as he had always done. After a number of years of life, he'd learned a couple of things. No one gets one hundred percent support and agreement. And everyone will always have one or more social haters in life. What was about to happen could possibly become negative fuel for such a hater.

Dr. Raheem Ali Gardner had been an inductee into the martial arts Hall of Fame in more than one worldwide governing organization over a number of years. He was nominated for another prestigious

Hall of Fame award. More than two hundred votes were tallied from all over the United States, including Alaska and Hawaii. When all were counted he had the largest number and became supreme grand master in 2014. He was recognized for his lifetime of achievement in the worldwide community. His first school had been at the Schofield Barracks in Hawaii (1977–1981); the second was in Bremerhaven, Germany (1984–1987); the third at Kumite in the Middle East (January 2011–present). The black-tie award ceremony was held at the Conference Center in College Park, Atlanta, Georgia on September 6, 2014. Many of the top US martial artists and martial art film stars were in attendance. He was overwhelmed by this induction, beyond anything he could have ever imagined.

Who among us can counsel God Almighty as to those in whom He finds delight? The only thing that one can say is "May He continue to bless you."

If you say "Newark," people from all over the world will automatically think *New Jersey*. The metropolitan media, or mind-benders, have historically broadcast the notion that many Newark residents are lazy and shiftless. The images that young people have been fed for some time feature high school drop-outs and passionate lovers of welfare. Dr. Gardner would never claim to be a perfect man. Examining his life closely, we see a great source of inspiration for young people. He makes a pretty decent living working for himself. So many things had to fall perfectly into place to make many of his realities possible. The slightest variation of any kind and we would be looking at a different life. When the Lord our God has something to say, he sometimes uses the least likely candidates to help make his point.

Dr. Raheem Ali Gardner's family supported him and put up with his high-octane sign-kicking antics. On the corner of Schuyler and Ecker, that sign would sound like Big Ben ringing in London. His little brother Cory had just come into this world. Shelia and Stacey provided a lot of love and huge belief in their older brother. His grandmother had the crucial job of praying for Raheem and everybody else she could possibly think of. Mother Gardner would look him square in the eye and say, "Son, I can only give you what it is I have. You will have to go out and do what you gotta do." Her firm message would serve as fuel to propel his remarkable train ride. The lifestyle provided by the city of Newark, New Jersey, along with his martial arts training, can be likened to the biblical phase "Iron sharpens iron."

Strengthen your minds, pull your pants up, and know that God has made your soil very fertile. The streets you see no hope in have produced champions and giants! Do not be afraid. Go out and do what you gotta do!

Dr. Raheem Ali Gardner's legacy will live on for many years to come. He will be known throughout the world. Raheem was introduced to an overwhelming lifestyle called martial arts. He certainly made some mistakes along the way. The state allowed him to escape some harsh consequences, and he would learn and grow from his experiences. Dr. Gardner knew that young people are going to stray from the family values that many are still being taught. Dr. Gardner would never endorse or encourage the use of any illegal drugs. His hope and vision is for young people to learn from his imperfections. He does not want young people to use drugs. His desire is that some may use his life examples as a sort of cheat sheet. "Life is going to be a test; do not choose my wrong answers. Pick the right answers, and allow God to be the true source of your inspiration."

Dr. Gardner goes far beyond the boundaries of sharing Martial Arts Instructions to his students. When you are entrusted with the character development of so many people your words really matter. If you are sincere in your quest to find GOD, here is what you may experience. His will for you is petitioned, then you make known your dreams and ambitions. Your spiritual eyes and ears will start to grow and develop. Raheem has come to learn that each day you wake up is much more than a flesh deal. In your area of pursuing that 10th degree Black Belt, it may take quite some time. The town you come from might not have such a good reputation, but you can still succeed. GOD, can grant you favor. Talking a good game is not going to cut it, your deeds have to line up. In the correct spirit of what is good and honorable go out and prove them wrong!

Credits:

Grand Master Raheem Ali Gardner
Grand Master William A. Wilson
Grand Master Eugene Floyd
Grand Master Jackie Cotton
Grand Master Turhan Bey
Master Malik
Mr. Jerome Hardgrove
Minister Diane Beckwith
Mr. James Bond
Mr. Roscoe Gray
Mrs. Viola Green
Mr. Tyris Henry
Mr. Ronnie Jones
Mr. Dereck Pierce
Mr. Chauncey Vandivet
Ms. Cheryl Williams

Hawthorne Avenue School photo provided by Principal

Printed in the United States
By Bookmasters